Countries Around the World

France

Mary Colson

Heinemann Library
Chicago, Illinois

www.heinemannraintree.com
Visit our website to find out
more information about
Heinemann-Raintree books.

To order:

☎ Phone 888-454-2279

🖥 Visit www.heinemannraintree.com
to browse our catalog and order online.

Edited by Louise Galpine, Kate DeVilliers, and Laura Knowles
Designed by Richard Parker
Original illustrations © Capstone Global Library Ltd 2011
Illustrated by Oxford Designers & Illustrators
Picture research by Liz Alexander
Originated by Capstone Global Library Ltd
Printed in China by CTPS

15 14 13 12 11
10 9 8 7 6 5 4 3 2 1

Library of Congress Cataloging-in-Publication Data
Colson, Mary.
  France / Mary Colson.
    p. cm.—(Countries around the world)
  Includes bibliographical references and index.
  ISBN 978-1-4329-5203-7 (hc)—ISBN 978-1-4329-5228-0 (pb) 1.
France—Juvenile literature. 2. France—History—Juvenile literature.
I. Title.
  DC17.C65 2012
  944—dc22   2010044771

Acknowledgments
We would like to thank the following for permission to reproduce
photographs: Alamy p. **12** (© Photos 12); Corbis pp. **10** (© The
Gallery Collection), **24** (© POOL/Reuters), **33** (© Tim De Waele/
TDWsport.com), **35** (© Riviere/photocuisine); Getty Images pp. **21**
(David C Tomlinson/Photographer's Choice), **29** (Sylvain Sonnet/
Photographer's Choice); iStockphoto pp. **9** (© Chris Dawson),
15 (© Christoph Achenbach), **27** (© Paul Fawcett); Photolibrary
pp. **6** (R H Productions), **7** (peter schickert), **18** (Alain Le Bot/
Photononstop), **20** (Henry Ausloos), **23** (Stéphane Ouzounoff),
30 (Ernst Wrba); Shutterstock pp. **5** (© Jean-Edouard Rozey),
8 (© Worakit Sirijinda), **17** (© PHB.cz (Richard Semik)), **26**
(© Baloncici), **31** (© Mikhail Zahranichny), **37** (© Paul Reid),
46 (© Route66), **34** (© PixAchi).

Cover photograph of tourists with red umbrellas near the Eiffel
Tower reproduced with permission of Corbis/© Owen Franken.

We would like to thank Rob Bowden for his invaluable help in the
preparation of this book.

Every effort has been made to contact copyright holders of material
reproduced in this book. Any omissions will be rectified in
subsequent printings if notice is given to the publisher.

Disclaimer
All the Internet addresses (URLs) given in this book were valid at
the time of going to press. However, due to the dynamic nature of
the Internet, some addresses may have changed, or sites may have
changed or ceased to exist since publication. While the author
and publisher regret any inconvenience this may cause readers, no
responsibility for any such changes can be accepted by either the
author or the publisher.

Contents

Introducing France 4

History: Romans, Revolution, Republic 6

Regions and Resources: Landscape and Living.............14

Wildlife: Protecting Nature...20

Infrastructure: Politics and People 24

Culture: Art, Music, and Leisure...30

France Today 36

Fact File 38

Timeline 40

Glossary 42

Find Out More...44

Topic Tools...46

Index 48

Some words are printed in bold, **like this**. You can find out what they mean by looking in the glossary.

Introducing France

What comes into your mind when you think of France? Do you see the Eiffel Tower and art galleries? Do you think of delicious cakes and cheese, or designer clothes?

France is the largest country in Western Europe and is famous as an artistic, stylish, and cultural nation with fantastic art, great literature, and fine wines. The landscape is equally impressive with dramatic mountains, deep river gorges, rugged coastlines, and beautiful beaches.

Politics and power

France is one of the places where the European Parliament meets, and is at the heart of European politics. It is a member of the **G8** group of wealthiest countries. France once had an **empire**, which included land in North and South America, Africa, and in the Pacific. The national flag is called the Tricolore and is three vertical stripes of blue, white, and red.

Language guardians

The *Académie Française* protects French **culture** and language. There are strict laws to ensure that most TV programs are French language in origin and not subtitled or **dubbed** from other languages.

How to say...

French people greet each other by kissing on both cheeks. French people say "*bonjour*" as a general greeting to other people, for example when they go into a shop.

good day	*bonjour*	(bon-jure)
how are you?	*ça va?*	(sa va)
I'm fine, thanks	*ça va bien, merci*	(sa va bee-an, mur-see)
my name is…	*Je m'appelle…*	(juh map-el)
see you later	*a tout à l'heure*	(a toot a ler)
bye	*au revoir*	(oh re-vwa)

France is truly spectacular. Villages perched on hilltops look out over deep valleys and farmland.

History: Romans, Revolution, Republic

France is named after the Franks, a **tribe** of people who lived in central Europe. Their ruler, Clovis (around 466–511 CE), went to war against the Romans and eventually reigned over what is now France. He also changed his religious beliefs and became a **Roman Catholic**.

Expanding empire

By the 900s CE, the Franks governed most of Belgium, the Netherlands, and parts of western Germany. In 1066, the French nobleman William of Normandy invaded England. He defeated the English king Harold II at the Battle of Hastings and was crowned king of England on Christmas Day.

From 1066 until 1558, France and England fought over French land and the throne. One of the most famous battles during this time was the Battle of Agincourt, won by England in 1415. In 1558, France regained Calais, the last French port held by the English. The two countries have remained separate ever since.

The Bayeux Tapestry tells the story of the Norman conquest of England in 1066.

The Romans built this amphitheater in the town of Orange. Plays and concerts are still performed there today.

Faith wars

In the 1500s, French Catholics and **Protestants** fought each other over their faith. In 1572, the Catholic queen ordered a day of killing known as the St. Bartholomew's Day **Massacre**. Hundreds of Protestants were killed. In 1598, the **Edict** of Nantes granted religious freedom.

Daily life

Throughout the 1600s and 1700s, poor families survived by working as farm laborers or as servants in the **chateaux** of the rich. Even children were sent out to work. In the evenings, women did sewing work to earn a few extra coins to help feed their family.

Cultural and political revolutions

The 1700s was a golden era in French art and science. It was a period of **extravagance** for the French **monarchy**. King Louis XIV had a luxurious palace built at Versailles.

Louis's grandson, Louis XVI, spent even more money. An unfair **tax** system meant that poorer workers paid the most, while the richer **nobles** paid little or no tax. A dangerous feeling of unrest was growing among the poor.

The Palace of Versailles is just outside Paris.

Daily life

The winter of 1788–1789 was especially cold. Frozen rivers stopped people from transporting food. The cost of food rose dramatically, and people were starving. By July, their anger had reached boiling point.

Long live the republic!

The night of July 14, 1789, changed France forever. Thousands of angry peasants marched through the streets of Paris crying out "Freedom!" and "Equality!" They stormed the hated Bastille prison and freed the prisoners inside. It was the start of the French Revolution.

The French Revolution was a battle for equal rights for everyone. The poor wanted a **republic**, which is a country with an **elected** government and no king or queen. The rich wanted to keep their privileged lifestyles and avoid taxes. Thousands of rich and poor died during the bloody revolution. Louis XVI and his queen Marie-Antoinette were executed by **guillotine** in 1793, along with many other nobles.

Bastille Day is on July 14. It is a public holiday in France.

An emperor and an empire

After the revolution, there was a **power vacuum** in France. In 1799, General Napoleon Bonaparte seized control. Napoleon was a military **genius**. He had spent much of his early army career abroad in Italy and Egypt helping to expand the French **Empire**. Once in power, he changed the tax system to make it fairer.

Empire building

In 1804, Napoleon crowned himself emperor and began creating a vast empire. Between 1804 and 1811, French armies gained territory in Africa, North America, and Europe. Emperor Napoleon seemed unstoppable.

This painting of Napoleon Bonaparte shows him leading his troops over the Alps into Italy.

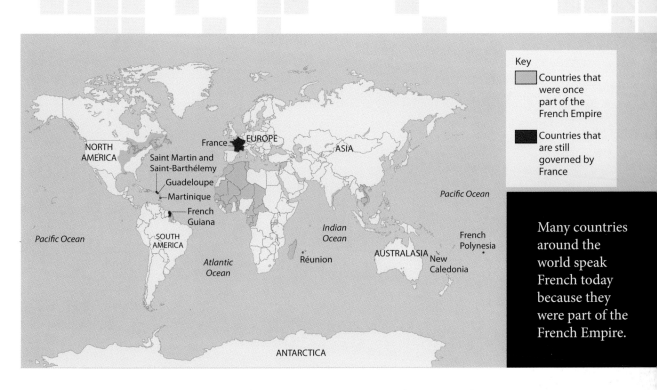

Key
- ■ Countries that were once part of the French Empire
- ■ Countries that are still governed by France

NORTH AMERICA

France EUROPE

ASIA

Saint Martin and Saint-Barthélemy

Guadeloupe

Martinique

French Guiana

Pacific Ocean

SOUTH AMERICA

Atlantic Ocean

Pacific Ocean

Indian Ocean

Réunion

AUSTRALASIA New Caledonia

French Polynesia

ANTARCTICA

Many countries around the world speak French today because they were part of the French Empire.

Other European countries, such as Great Britain, were determined to stop Napoleon's plans. A series of wars led to Napoleon's eventual defeat at the Battle of Waterloo in 1815. Napoleon was **exiled** to the Mediterranean island of St. Helena, and Louis XVIII, brother of the executed Louis XVI, took the throne.

France continued as a monarchy until 1848, when a series of bloody revolutions across Europe saw working people demand equal rights and political change. By 1900, despite political upheaval and social unrest, France had expanded into Southeast Asia and the Pacific islands. The empire was still growing.

VICTOR HUGO (1802–1885)

Victor Hugo was a poet, playwright, and novelist. He wrote the story of *The Hunchback of Notre Dame*. He also wrote *Les Misérables*, which is set in the time leading up to the 1848 revolution. The story has been turned into a world-famous musical.

War and peace

In the last 100 years, French **culture** has influenced global fashion, movies, and science. French people, though, have twice witnessed the horrors of war on their own soil.

During World War I (1914–1918) many battles were fought in **trenches**. At the Battle of the Somme, over 700,000 soldiers died. Great Britain, the United States, and other European countries helped defeat Germany in 1918.

Daily life

Life in the trenches was a daily fight for survival. Soldiers had to dodge **sniper** bullets, enemy bombs, and diseases carried by thousands of rats. Lice bred in their dirty clothes and caused unbearable itching. The cold and wet conditions also caused **trench foot**. If untreated, it could result in **amputation**.

During World War II, French Resistance fighters blew up railroads to disrupt German supply lines.

LUCIE AUBRAC (1912-2007)

Lucie Aubrac was a member of the French Resistance. She helped to run the secret newspaper *Libération (Freedom)*. This told people what the Resistance was doing to fight the Germans.

In 1939, World War II began. In 1940, Adolf Hitler's German forces conquered Paris. The north and west parts of France were occupied until 1944. Secretly, General Charles de Gaulle organized the **Resistance** movement from London. When the war ended in 1945, de Gaulle briefly became leader of France, and later was president from 1959 to 1969.

A new direction

In the second half of the 1900s, many of France's **colonies**, such as Algeria and Vietnam, gained independence. Today, France no longer has an empire. Many people from its former colonies come to live in France, making it a very **multicultural** country.

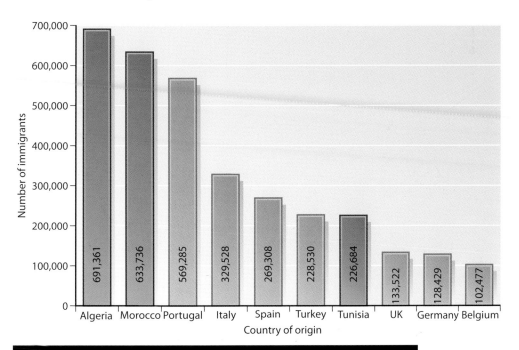

This bar chart shows the top ten countries that immigrants living in France have come from, based on a survey in 2006. The red bars represent former French colonies.

Regions and Resources: Landscape and Living

France is a diverse country with mountains, beaches, **dormant** volcanoes, and fertile farmland. Over a quarter of the country is forest. There are five mountain ranges, including the Alps, the Pyrenees, and the Massif Central, a spectacular chain of extinct volcanoes. Mont Blanc in the Alps is Europe's highest mountain at 15,780 feet (4,810 meters).

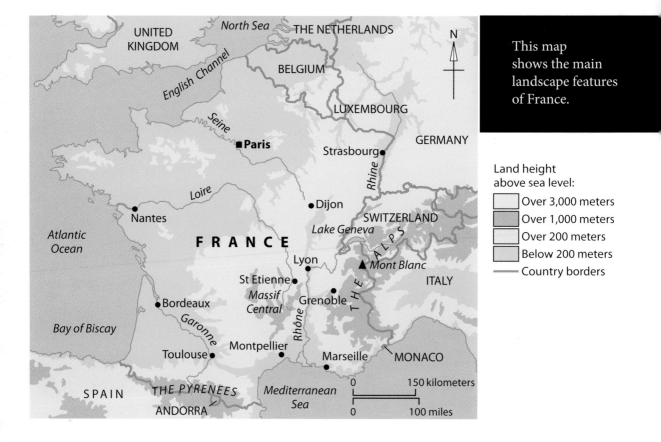

This map shows the main landscape features of France.

Land height above sea level:
- Over 3,000 meters
- Over 1,000 meters
- Over 200 meters
- Below 200 meters
- Country borders

Weather report

The French climate is mild, with monthly averages between 37 and 66°F (3 and 19°C). The north is cooler than the south, with the Alps the coldest place in winter. Along the Mediterranean coast, summer temperatures are high, making this area one of Europe's most popular vacation destinations.

Dormant volcanoes in the Massif Central make very fertile farmland and forests.

Neighbors and numbers

Bordered by Spain, Germany, Italy, Belgium, Switzerland, Monaco, Andorra, and Luxembourg, France is home to 64 million people who live in about 210,000 square miles (550,000 square kilometers) of land. Because of its shape, France is also known as "the hexagon."

France governs four countries overseas. They are French Guiana, Martinique, Guadaloupe, and Réunion.

There are five main rivers in France. The longest river is the Loire at 634 miles (1,020 kilometers), followed by the Rhine, the Rhône, the Seine, and the Garonne. The four seas around the coast are the Mediterranean, the North Sea, the English Channel, and the Atlantic Ocean.

How to say...

river	*la fleuve*	(la flerve)
beach	*la plage*	(la plarge)
mountain	*la montagne*	(la montan)
sea	*la mer*	(la mair)
lake	*le lac*	(luh lak)
forest	*la forêt*	(la foray)
coast	*la côte*	(la cot)
valley	*la vallée*	(la valay)

Regional character

France is divided into 22 administrative regions, which are then divided into smaller *departements*. The richest region is the Ile-de-France, which includes Paris. Each region has its own character, traditions, cuisine, and flag. Some have their own **dialect**. In Brittany, some people speak Breton.

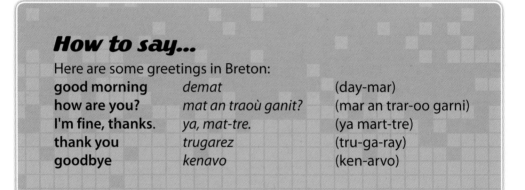

How to say...

Here are some greetings in Breton:

good morning	*demat*	(day-mar)
how are you?	*mat an traoù ganit?*	(mar an trar-oo garni)
I'm fine, thanks.	*ya, mat-tre.*	(ya mart-tre)
thank you	*trugarez*	(tru-ga-ray)
goodbye	*kenavo*	(ken-arvo)

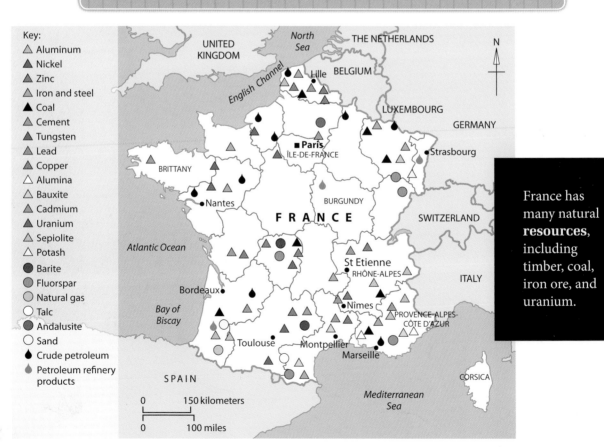

Key:
△ Aluminum
▲ Nickel
▲ Zinc
△ Iron and steel
▲ Coal
△ Cement
▲ Tungsten
△ Lead
△ Copper
△ Alumina
△ Bauxite
△ Cadmium
▲ Uranium
△ Sepiolite
△ Potash
● Barite
◐ Fluorspar
○ Natural gas
○ Talc
● Andalusite
○ Sand
⬤ Crude petroleum
⬤ Petroleum refinery products

France has many natural **resources**, including timber, coal, iron ore, and uranium.

These sunflower fields are in Provence, in southern France.

A nation of farmers

Different regions specialize in different crops, depending on climate and soil. Brittany is the main vegetable-growing region, while Rhône-Alps is a key dairy-farming area. The vineyards that make French wine are mostly in Burgundy and Bordeaux. Sunny Provence is the main flower, olive, and orchard area.

Factory towns

The industrial centers of France are mainly in the north and center. Large chemical factories, textile mills, and food processing plants dominate the towns of Lille, Paris, and St. Etienne. Nîmes, in the south, has a large cloth industry, and is where denim comes from. The word *denim* means "de Nîmes" or "from Nîmes."

Daily life

In the cities, people mostly live in tall, modern blocks of apartments. In the countryside, where there is more space, people often build their own houses. In the mountains, people live in traditional wooden chalets. Many houses have shutters outside the windows for extra security and to keep the rooms inside cool.

17

Economic status

France has one of the largest **economies** in the world, worth over $2.1 trillion per year. It is in the eurozone of 16 European countries that use the euro as **currency**. The symbol of the euro is €. The average yearly income per person in France is around $33,300.

Industrial strength

France has a workforce of 28 million people. Large employers include the national airline, Air France, and car companies Renault and Peugeot. The world's largest airliner, the Airbus 380, is built in France. French factories produce 250,000 cars every month.

High-tech factories employ thousands of French engineers. In this one they are building part of an airplane.

YOUNG PEOPLE

In 2010, one in four people between the ages of 16 and 25 was unemployed. The government is trying to help by paying employers to take on apprentices, so young people can get skills and work experience.

Trade: buying and selling

France's most important trading partners are the United Kingdom, Germany, Spain, and Italy. France **imports** and **exports** machinery and equipment, cars, crude oil, aircraft, textiles, plastics, and chemicals.

France fared better than most large economies with the global **credit crunch** that began in 2008, but there were still job losses. Overall unemployment in France remains at 9.1 percent, which is higher than the European average of 8.2 percent.

Gross Domestic Product (GDP) is the total amount of goods or services made in a country in a year. This pie chart shows what business types are important to the French economy, such as tourism. France is the most visited country in the world, with 75 million tourists every year.

Agriculture
1.8%

Industry
19.3%

Services
78.9%

Wildlife: Protecting Nature

France has large areas of relatively unspoiled **habitat** that supports a wide range of native wildlife.

High up in the rocky Alps lives the Alpine ibex. This wild goat can defend itself against predators such as wolves with its long, curved horns. In the early 1900s, the Alpine ibex was nearly hunted to **extinction**, but it is now protected by law.

Horses of the marsh

Camargue horses have lived wild in the marshes of the Camargue region in the south of France for thousands of years. The horses are small, sturdy, and tough. They are born brown or black and become white as they get older.

Camargue horses are protected and each new birth is registered.

The beautiful waterways and coast of the Calanques are due to become a national park in 2011.

Conservation success

The mountains of the Pyrenees in southwest France are home to the Pyrenean brown bear. The bear was hunted to near extinction in the 1990s, but it was reintroduced in 1996 when three bears were brought from Slovenia. The bears have been **breeding** successfully, and there are now believed to be about 15 brown bears in the mountains.

National parks

There are six national parks in mainland France, covering two percent of the country and attracting over seven million visitors every year. Vanoise National Park in the Alps was created in 1963 and covers 204 square miles (528 square kilometers). It is free to enter national parks in France.

How to say...

cat	le chat	(luh sha)
dog	le chien	(luh she-ann)
wolf	le loup	(luh loo)
boar	le sanglier	(luh son-glee-eh)
rabbit	le lapin	(luh lap-an)
bird	l'oiseau	(lwa-zo)
horse	le cheval	(luh sheval)
eagle	l'aigle	(leg-la)
bear	l'ours	(lawss)

Environmental awareness

Like many **industrialized** countries, France has its share of environmental problems. Acid rain harms the country's forests, while factories and vehicle **emissions** cause air pollution in the cities. In the countryside, agricultural chemicals, such as fertilizers, run off the fields and pollute rivers. Strict environmental protection laws are now in place. These aim to cut carbon emissions and limit water and air pollution.

Daily life

The French public are very aware of environmental issues. Most shops sell drinks in glass bottles that can be returned for refilling. Supermarkets charge for plastic bags, so shoppers take their own reusable ones. All towns and cities have recycling bins for glass, paper, cans, and **landfill** waste.

Powering the nation

Most of France's electricity comes from nuclear power. There are 58 nuclear power plants all over the country. Nuclear power is clean to **generate**, but it produces highly **toxic** waste.

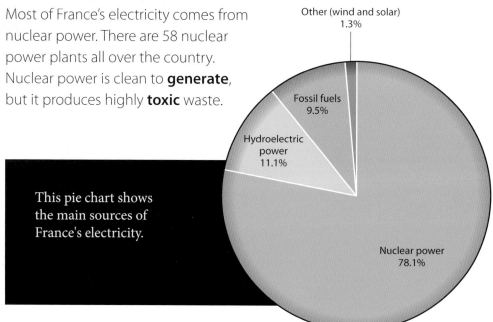

This pie chart shows the main sources of France's electricity.

Other (wind and solar)
1.3%

Fossil fuels
9.5%

Hydroelectric
power
11.1%

Nuclear power
78.1%

Most of France's electricity comes from nuclear power stations.

How to say...

Earth	*la terre*	(la tair)
nature	*la nature*	(la na-teur)
the environment	*l'environnement*	(lon-veer-onnamon)
global warming	*le réchauffement climatique*	(luh ray-shorfmon kleemateek)
polluted water	*l'eau polluée*	(low pol-loo-way)
recycling	*le recyclage*	(luh re-seek-larg)
pollution	*la pollution*	(la polooshun)
green	*vert*	(vair)

Infrastructure:
Politics and People

The French parliament consists of two houses: the Senate with 348 **elected** members, and the National Assembly with 577. Senators serve six-year terms, while the National Assembly is elected every five years. The National Assembly meets at the Palais Bourbon in central Paris.

Political parties

The four main political parties are the Socialist party, the conservative Rassemblement pour la République, the Union pour la Democratie Française, and the French Communist party.

The president leads the government, and he or she is **voted** in for a five-year term. The president then appoints the prime minister. The voting age is 18 in France.

The Elysée Palace in Paris is the official residence of the French president.

Part of Europe

France is one of 27 countries in the **European Union (EU)**. The EU is a political and economic union with an elected parliament. There are many common **policies** across Europe dealing with **trade** and defense. EU law allows people to move, travel, and work easily in other member countries.

YOUNG PEOPLE

The European Youth Parliament (EYP) has many different committees across Europe, including one in France. The EYP offers young people between ages 16 and 22 a chance to express their opinions on political and topical issues. Students are encouraged to debate, think independently, and find solutions to problems.

Health care

When French people are ill, they go to the doctor. They pay for the consultation and claim the costs back on their **health insurance**. French employees pay about 20 percent of their salary to fund the **social security system**. The World Health Organization (WHO) ranks France's health care system as the world's best.

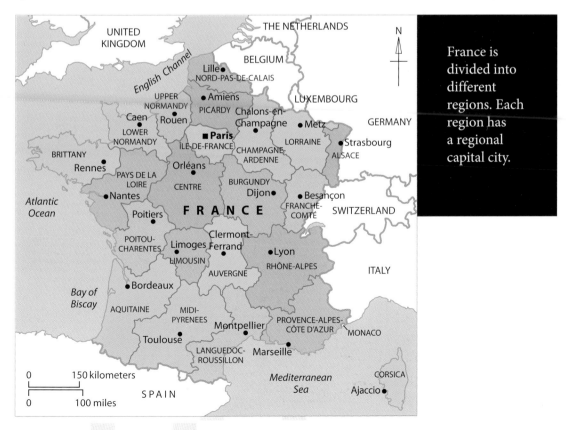

France is divided into different regions. Each region has a regional capital city.

Getting around

France has some challenging land for road builders and engineers. The Alps and Pyrenees have many tunnels through the mountains, as well as zig-zagging roads up to the high ski resorts.

Autoroutes are the motorways that cross the country, mainly from north to south. To travel on most of these, people pay a toll. The cost depends on how far the driver has traveled. In France, cars drive on the right, like in the U.S.

Beating the traffic

In Paris and other large cities, such as Lyon and Marseille, there is a Metro (underground) system. The Metro helps to prevent traffic jams and reduce air pollution. In Paris, many people use the *bateau-bus* (boat-bus) that travels to different stops along the River Seine.

Daily life

Traffic jams in Paris have been eased by a bicycle rental plan. There are *vélib* stations (short for *vélo-libre* or "bike freedom") all over the city, with more than 20,000 bikes in use. Cyclists pay for the time they use the bike and can return the bike to any station.

It takes 2 hours 15 minutes to travel the 307 miles (495 kilometers) from Paris to London on the Eurostar. The trains go under the sea in a tunnel and travel at 186 mph (300 kph).

At 1,125 feet (343 meters), the Millau Viaduct is the world's tallest vehicle bridge. The Eiffel Tower could fit underneath it!

Transportation in France	
Railroads	20,000 miles
Roads	556,000 miles
Canals	5,300 miles
Number of airports	41 (of any major size)
Number of private cars	469 per 1,000 people

Waterways

All over France, rivers and canals are used to transport industrial goods by barge. The main rivers are the Rhone, the Seine, the Garonne, and the Loire. The main canals are the Canal de Bourgogne, the Canal du Rhin au Rhone, and the Canal de la Marne au Rhin.

School life

Nearly all children in France attend schools funded by the government. Classes begin at 8:30 a.m. and finish around 4:30 p.m. There is no school on Wednesday afternoons, because children play sports or have music classes then. Many schools have lessons on Saturday mornings.

School is **compulsory** between the ages of six and sixteen. Children learn French, history, geography, social studies, math, science, art, and music. Children also learn English or another foreign language.

How to say...

French	*le français*	(luh fronsay)
English	*l'anglais*	(long-glay)
social studies	*les sciences sociales*	(lay sea-ons so-see-arl)
art	*l'art*	(lar)
chemistry	*la chimie*	(la shimee)
history	*l'histoire*	(listwah)
geography	*la géo(graphie)*	(la jayograffie)
math	*les mathématiques*	(lay mat-eh-mateek)
music	*la musique*	(la moozeek)

Daily life

The school lunch break lasts for two hours. Students go home to eat with their families or eat in the school cafeteria. Lunch always has three courses: salad or soup, a main course, and then cheese or dessert.

French children don't wear school uniforms.

Higher education

After elementary school, students go to a *collége* from the age of 11 to 15, and then go on to a *lycée*. Students can leave school at 16 to find work, or they can stay until they are 18 and study for the *baccalauréate* exam to go to a university. French universities have high standards, and many students come to study from other French-speaking nations.

Culture: Art, Music, and Leisure

French **culture** is associated with style, from the art museums and fashion catwalks of Paris, to the glamorous Cannes Film Festival.

Capital of culture

Paris has more than 70 museums, famous landmarks like the Eiffel Tower and Notre Dame cathedral, and thousands of cafés. The Musée d'Orsay has a large collection of paintings by the Impressionists.

THE IMPRESSIONISTS

In the late 1800s, a new style of painting began. Impressionist painters studied the effect that light had on their subjects, and they then tried to paint it. Claude Monet, Berthe Morisot, and Auguste Renoir are famous Impressionists.

Sitting in a café is part of daily life in Paris.

The *Mona Lisa* by Leonardo da Vinci is in the Louvre.

Musical figures

France has produced many **classical** composers, such as Claude Debussy, who wrote "Clair de Lune," and Camille Saint-Saëns, who wrote *The Carnival of the Animals*. Other popular French musicians include the nightclub singer, Edith Piaf.

EDITH PIAF (1915–1963)

Edith Piaf was known as the "little sparrow" because she was only 4 feet 7 inches (142 centimeters) tall. Her songs reflected her experiences. Her most famous song is "Je ne regrette rien," which means "I regret nothing."

Book club

France has a great tradition of literature. Emile Zola and Gustave Flaubert wrote about people's lives and their problems. Molière wrote comic plays poking fun at the upper classes, and Alexandre Dumas created swashbuckling heroes, such as the Three Musketeers.

Lights, camera, action!

In 1895 the Lumière brothers invented the portable movie camera, and cinema was born. The French movie industry has been making successful movies for over 100 years. In 2008, Marion Cotillard won an Oscar for playing Edith Piaf in *La Vie en Rose*. Every year, film stars from around the world attend the Cannes Film Festival and compete to win the Palme d'Or prize for best movie.

FRENCH AUTHORS

French writers have written many classic children's stories. *The Little Prince* by Antoine de Saint Exupéry and *Babar the Elephant* by Jean de Brunhoff have been translated into many languages. The most famous stories are by Charles Perrault, who was one of the first to publish fairy tales. "Sleeping Beauty," "Cinderella," and "Little Red Riding Hood" are loved by children all over the world.

National holidays

By law, every French **citizen** can take five weeks of annual vacation. On top of this, there are 11 national holidays each year, including Bastille Day. Many banks, stores, and museums close on these days.

Sporting nation

Popular sports in France include rugby, soccer, tennis, and a lawn bowling game called *boules*. Climbing, hiking, and skiing are popular in the mountains.

The Tour de France is one of the biggest annual sporting events in the world. International teams of cyclists pedal over 2,237 miles (3,600 kilometers) around the country in three weeks, riding up huge mountains in the Alps and the Pyrenees. The race always finishes in Paris.

Thousands of fans line the route to cheer on the cyclists in the Tour de France.

Food and drink

France is famous for wine, cheese, and fine food. The country has the world's second largest area of vineyards, which produce between seven and eight billion bottles of wine a year, including over 320 million bottles of champagne.

Regional food

Each region has its own food specialities. For example, in the Alps, fondu is popular. This is a shared pot of melted cheese with wine, into which people dip bread, meat, and vegetables on long skewers. Across the country, over 1,000 different types of cheese are made.

Many French shoppers buy food from specialist shops. *Boulangeries* open very early in the morning to sell fresh bread and croissants. *Charcuteries* sell sausages and patés, and *pâtisseries* sell cakes.

Festival food

French fries and French toast are well known, but what about snails in garlic butter and lightly fried frogs' legs? These **delicacies** are eaten as special treats, usually at Christmas.

French crèpes

Ask an adult to help you make this delicious treat.

Ingredients

- 1 cup all-purpose flour
- 1 teaspoon white sugar
- ¼ teaspoon salt
- 3 eggs
- 2 cups milk
- 2 tablespoons butter, melted
- sugar and lemon juice to serve

What to do

1. Sift together the flour, sugar, and salt in a bowl.
2. In a different bowl, beat the eggs and milk together.
3. Add the flour mixture to the eggs and stir in the melted butter to make a batter.
4. Heat a lightly oiled frying pan over medium-high heat.
5. Pour 2 tablespoons of batter into the pan for each crèpe.
6. Tip and turn the pan to spread the batter as thinly as possible. Brown on both sides.
7. Serve hot with sugar and lemon juice.

France Today

France is a country that captures the imagination. From the romance of Paris to the splendor of its **chateaux**, the country's artistic **culture** has produced writers and artists who have made their mark on the world. The country's historic buildings, food, and spectacular landscape ensure that millions of people visit each year.

Modern life

France today has a vibrant **multicultural** society with a strong sense of its own history and pride in its traditions. Many people from its former **colonies** come to live and work in France, adding to the cultural mix.

YOUNG PEOPLE

French teenagers like to keep up with the latest electronic gadgets. It is fashionable to have a *téléphone portable* (cell phone), a *baladeur* (MP3 player), and an *ordinateur portable* (laptop). They also *surfer l'Internet*. There are cyber cafés in most towns, as only 52 percent of French homes have Internet access.

Political progression

France is taking a lead within European politics and on the global stage. As a permanent member of the **United Nations Security Council**, France works closely with other countries to find solutions to international problems, such as war and terrorism.

The future

France is a country that doesn't stand still. It's always changing and developing in order to improve the quality of life for its **citizens**. It's a country that embraces new technology and design. However, French history, language, and identity remain very important to its people as the country moves into the future.

The Grand Arch de la Defense in Paris is in the country's ultra-modern business and banking district.

Fact File

Official language:	French
Capital city:	Paris
Bordering countries:	Andorra, Belgium, Germany, Italy, Luxembourg, Monaco, Spain, Switzerland
Population:	64 million (2 million overseas)
Largest cities in terms of population:	Paris, Lyon, Marseille
Life expectancy at birth:	77.91 years for men; 84.44 years for women
Religions:	**Roman Catholic**: up to 88%, **Protestant**: 2%, Jewish: 1%, Muslim: up to 10%, other/none: 4%
National flower:	lily (fleur de lys)
Area:	212,935 square miles (551,500 square kilometers)
Major rivers:	Seine, Somme, Rhône, Garonne, Loire
Highest point:	Mont Blanc, in the Alps, at 15,780 feet (4,810 meters)
Currency:	euro (100 cents = 1 euro)
Natural resources:	coal, iron ore, uranium, arsenic, timber, fish
Imports:	machinery and equipment, vehicles, crude oil, aircraft, plastics, chemicals
Exports:	machinery and transportation equipment, aircraft, plastics, chemicals, pharmaceutical products, iron and steel, beverages
Major industries:	aerospace engineering, chemicals, tourism
Literacy rates:	99 percent of the population can read and write
Climate:	temperate continental
Membership of international organizations:	**G8**, UN Security Council, **European Union**, eurozone
Units of measurement:	metric

World Heritage Sites:	32 **World Heritage Sites** including Palace of Versailles, bridge of Avignon, banks of the Seine in Paris, Notre Dame cathedral, Loire valley chateaux
Famous inventions:	Braille (1824), aspirin (1853)
Other territories administered by France:	Martinique, Guadeloupe, French Guiana, Réunion. There are 29 countries and regions around the world that have French as an official language, including the Canadian province of Quebec, Algeria, Madagascar, Cameroon, and Vietnam.
Festivals:	Cannes Film Festival, the Menton lemon festival, the Paris Chocolate Show, Dijon's November food and wine fair
Famous French people:	Thierry Henry (soccer player), Richard Gasquet (tennis player), Montgolfier brothers (inventors), Lumière brothers (inventors), Claude Debussy (composer), Louis Pasteur (scientist), Berthe Morisot (artist), Claude Monet (artist), Victor Hugo (writer), Pierre Curie (scientist), Coco Chanel (designer), Brigitte Bardot (actor), Gérard Depardieu (actor)

French national anthem

The French National Anthem is called "La Marseillaise." It was written in 1792 by Claude Joseph Rouget de Lisle and was a revolutionary song to encourage the working classes to rise up against the **nobles**. This is the first verse:

Allons, enfants de la patrie,
Le jour de gloire est arrivé.
Contre nous, de la tyrannie,
L'étendard sanglant est levé;
l'étendard sanglant est levé.
Entendez-vous, dans les campagnes
Mugir ces féroces soldats?
Ils viennent jusque dans nos bras
Égorger nos fils, nos compagnes.
Aux armes, citoyens!

Come, children of the Fatherland,
The day of glory has arrived!
Against us, **Tyranny's**
Bloody banner is raised,
Do you hear in the countryside
Those ferocious soldiers roaring?
They come up to your arms
to cut the throats of our sons,
*   our comrades.*
To arms, citizens!

Timeline

CE is short for Common Era. CE is added after a date and means that the date occurred after the birth of Jesus Christ, for example, 720 CE.

1st–5th century CE	The region of Gaul (roughly the same area as modern France) is settled mainly by the Gauls, Celts, and Franks, and is under Roman rule
486 CE	Clovis I, leader of the Franks, conquers northern and central France. **Roman Catholicism** is adopted.
771 CE	Charlemagne (Charles the Great) unites more areas of France, as well as parts of northern Italy, Germany, and Spain
1066	William of Normandy invades England and takes the throne
around 1337	Edward III of England claims the French crown
1337	Beginning of the Hundred Years' War
1415	Battle of Agincourt. Henry V of England defeats French forces.
1558	Calais returns to French control, marking the end of English rule in France
1572	St. Bartholomew's Day **Massacre**
1598	**Edict** of Nantes means religious freedom for all
1635	Académie Française created
1643–1715	Reign of Louis XIV. France is the dominant power in Europe.
1682	Louis XIV establishes the royal court at the Palace of Versailles
1789	French Revolution
1792	National anthem, "La Marseillaise," is written
1799	Napoleon takes power
1803–14	Napoleon expands the French **Empire**
1804	Napoleon crowns himself Emperor
1809	The *baccalauréate* exam is created
1814	Napoleon is **exiled** to Elba

1815	Napoleon returns and is defeated at the Battle of Waterloo
1830–1848	Reign of Louis-Philippe
1889	Eiffel Tower is built
1895	Lumière brothers invent the portable movie camera
1903	First Tour de France takes place
1914–1918	World War I takes place
1939	Start of World War II
June 22, 1940	France surrenders to Nazi Germany. German occupation of France begins. The **Resistance** tries to disrupt German rule.
1944	France is freed from German occupation
1945	End of World War II
1946	First Cannes Film Festival
1979	European Parliament opens
1993	**European Union** is formed to ease **trade** and business among member states
1994	The Channel Tunnel opens, and Eurostar trains start running between Paris and London
1998	France hosts and wins the World Cup
January 1, 1999	France adopts the euro as its **currency**
2008	Marion Cotillard wins an Oscar for playing Edith Piaf in *La Vie en Rose*
2007–2010	The global **credit crunch** creates high youth unemployment in France

Glossary

amputation surgical removal of a limb

breed bear offspring; a word usually used for animals or birds

chateau (plural: chateaux) castle or large house

citizen legal resident of a country

classical serious, artistic music, often played by an orchestra or piano

colony country ruled from afar by another country

compulsory required by rules or law

credit crunch global economic problem caused when the cash flow or credit from banks stops and many businesses cannot get loans. This results in mass unemployment.

culture practices, traditions, and beliefs of a society

currency banknotes and coins accepted in exchange for goods and services

delicacy food that is expensive, hard to get, and highly thought of

dialect regional language

dormant not active or erupting

dubbed when a new soundtrack is added to a film or TV program, usually in a different language

economy to do with money and the industry and jobs in a country

edict official order

elect choose by voting. The public elects a person to represent them in parliament.

emissions gases released into the atmosphere from factories and homes

empire group of countries ruled by a single powerful country

European Union (EU) political and economic union of (currently) 27 European countries

exiled sent away and banned from your home country

export sell goods to another country

extinction dying out of a species

extravagance over-the-top spending or indulgence

G8 group of the eight richest countries in the world

generate produce

genius extremely clever person

guillotine device used to behead people

habitat environment where a plant or animal is found

health insurance money paid in advance for health protection

import buy goods from another country

industrialized well-developed production methods

landfill garbage that is buried underground in large areas called landfill sites

massacre deliberate killing of many people

monarch king or queen

multicultural mix of people from different cultures and countries

noble person belonging to a high and powerful social class

policy idea and course of action

power vacuum political situation created when there is no clear leader

Protestant Christian who practices their faith and doesn't follow the pope's leadership

republic country with an elected leader and no monarch

Resistance French freedom organization whose members fought against German occupation during Wolrd War II

resource means available for a country to develop, such as minerals and energy sources

Roman Catholic Christian who follows the beliefs of the Roman Catholic Church and the leadership of the pope

sniper marksman, sharpshooter

social security system government system of welfare ensuring that financial help is given to people in need

tax money paid by people to the government. Taxes can come from wages or be placed on goods that people buy.

toxic poisonous, extremely harmful to health

trade buying and selling of goods, usually between countries

trench long, narrow ditch in the ground used as shelter from enemy fire or attack

trench foot common problem for soldiers during World War I, caused by living in wet and cold trenches. Limited blood circulation to the foot results in decay.

tribe independent social group, historically often made up of primitive or nomadic people

tyranny very harsh, strict government

United Nations Security Council international committee of the world's most powerful nations devoted to maintaining world peace

vote choose. People vote for someone to win an election.

World Heritage Site special site of global importance

Find Out More

Books

Conboy, Fiona, and Roseline Ngcheong-Lum. *France*. New York: Benchmark Books, 2010.

De la Bedoyere, Camilla. *France in Our World*. Mankato, MN: Smart Apple Media, 2010.

Grack, Rachel. *France*. Minneapolis: Bellwether Media, 2010.

Hardyman, Robyn. *Celebrate! France*. New York: Chelsea House Publications, 2009.

Streissguth, Tom. *France*. Minneapolis: Lerner Publications, 2008.

Townsend, Sue. *France, revised edition* (A World of Recipes). Chicago: Heinemann-Raintree, 2009.

Websites

en.chateauversailles.fr/history-
Go to the Palace of Versailles website to learn more about the history of the French kings and queens, and where they lived.

us.franceguide.com
Visit the official website of the French Government Tourist Office to find out more about the different regions of France, things to do, and places to see.

www.bbc.co.uk/schools/primaryfrench
This website has interactive games and activities to help you learn French.

Places to visit

If you ever get the chance to go to France, here are some of the places you could visit:

Arc de Triomphe, Paris
Climb to the top of Napoleon's triumphal arch and look down the Champs-Elysées to the Louvre.

Caves de Niaux, Ariège
See prehistoric cave paintings and impressive rock formations in some of Europe's largest underground caverns.

Champs-Elysées, Paris
Walk up the grandest avenue in the capital.

Eiffel Tower, Paris
Walk to the first level or ride to the top to get fabulous views of Paris.

Futuroscope Park, Poitiers
Have fun at France's largest interactive science and technology park.

Louvre Museum, Paris
Explore this world-famous art museum and see the Mona Lisa.

Luberon Valley, Provence
See beautiful hilltop villages surrounded by fields of sunflowers and lavender.

Mer de Glace railroad and Aiguille du midi cable car, Chamonix
Since 1908, a train service has been taking tourists up to the incredible Mer de Glace glacier. After that ride, go 12,467 feet (3,800 meters) to the top of the Alps and see Mont Blanc up close!

Musee d'Orsay, Paris
See the large collection of Impressionist paintings at this museum.

Palace of Versailles, near Paris
Visit the home of the kings and queens of France and see the luxury in which they lived.

Tuillerie Gardens, Paris
Hang out with the locals in the capital's most central park.

Topic Tools

You can use these topic tools for your school projects. Trace the map onto a sheet of paper, using the thick black outline to guide you.

The French flag is called the *Tricolore*, or "three colors." It's easy to see why! Copy the flag design and then color in your picture. Make sure you use the right colors.

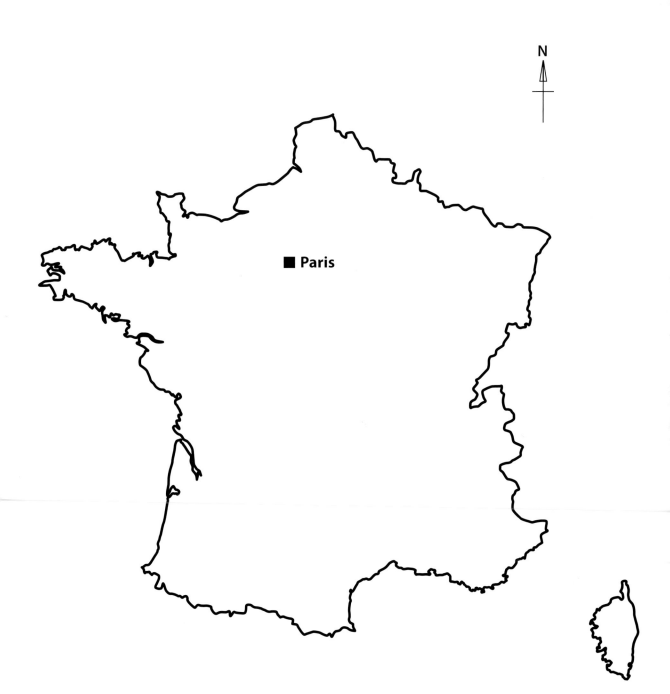

■ Paris

N

Index

Alps 14, 20, 21, 26
art 30
Aubrac, Lucie 13
autoroutes 26
average income 18

Bastille Day 9
Battle of Agincourt 6
Battle of Waterloo 11
bicycle rental plan 26
bordering countries 15, 38
Brittany 16, 17

Calanques 21
Camargue 20
canals 27
car ownership 27
Châtelet, Émilie du 8
climate 14
Clovis 6
coastline 15
colonies 13
culture 12, 30–35
currency 18

daily life 7, 12, 17, 22, 26, 28

economy 18
education 28–29
Elysée Palace 24
environmental issues 22
European Union (EU) 4, 25

famous French people 39
farming 17
festivals 39
food 34–35
Franks 6
French Empire 4, 6, 10, 11, 13

G8 group 4

Gaulle, Charles de 13
global recession 19
government 24
Grand Arch de la Defense 37
greetings 4
Gross Domestic Product (GDP) 19

health care 25
history 6–13, 40–41
Hugo, Victor 11

immigration 13
imports and exports 19, 38
Impressionist painters 30
industries 17, 18, 38
infrastructure 24–29

landscape 4, 5, 14
language 4, 15, 16, 21, 23, 28
life expectancy 38
literature 11, 31, 32
Louis XIV 8
Louvre 31

Marie-Antoinette, Queen 9
Massif Central 14, 15
Metro systems 26
Millau Viaduct 27
Mont Blanc 14
mountains 14
movie industry 32
multiculturalism 13, 36
music 31

Napoleon Bonaparte 10–11
national anthem 31, 39
national flag 4
national holidays 9, 32
national parks 21
natural resources 16, 38

Norman conquest of England 6
nuclear power 22, 23

Orange 7
overseas territories 15, 39

Paris 24, 26, 30, 31, 37
Piaf, Edith 31
population 38
Provence 17
Pyrenees 14, 21, 26

railroads 26, 27
recycling 22
regions 16, 17, 25
religion 6, 7, 38
Resistance movement 13
Revolution 9
rivers 15, 27, 38

schools 28–29
social security system 25
sports 32, 33

television 4
Tour de France 32, 33
tourism 19, 36
trade 19, 25
transportation 26–27

unemployment 19
United Nations 36
universities 29

Versailles 8

wildlife 20–21
William of Normandy 6
wines 17, 34
World Heritage Sites 39
World Wars I and II 12–13

young people 19, 25, 28–29, 36

Titles in the series

Afghanistan	978 1 4329 5195 5
Brazil	978 1 4329 5196 2
Chile	978 1 4329 5197 9
Costa Rica	978 1 4329 5198 6
Cuba	978 1 4329 5199 3
Czech Republic	978 1 4329 5200 6
England	978 1 4329 5201 3
Estonia	978 1 4329 5202 0
France	978 1 4329 5203 7
Germany	978 1 4329 5204 4
Haiti	978 1 4329 5205 1
Hungary	978 1 4329 5206 8
India	978 1 4329 5207 5
Iran	978 1 4329 5208 2
Iraq	978 1 4329 5209 9
Italy	978 1 4329 5210 5
Latvia	978 1 4329 5211 2
Lithuania	978 1 4329 5212 9
Mexico	978 1 4329 5213 6
Pakistan	978 1 4329 5214 3
Poland	978 1 4329 5215 0
Scotland	978 1 4329 5216 7
Wales	978 1 4329 5217 4
Yemen	978 1 4329 5218 1